About the Author

Dorothy Lockyer has been writing poetry throughout her life. This is her first attempt at writing specifically for children. Having worked with children for many years she feels she has a special affinity with them.

A previous book by Dorothy P. Lockyer is *Potpourri of Poetry* published by Austin Macauley.

A Pocket Full of Rhymes

Dorothy Lockyer

A Pocket Full of Rhymes

Olympia Publishers
London

www.olympiapublishers.com
OLYMPIA PAPERBACK EDITION

Copyright © Dorothy Lockyer 2019
Illustrations by Jon NcNaught

The right of Dorothy Lockyer to be identified as author of
this work has been asserted in accordance with sections 77 and 78 of the
Copyright, Designs and Patents Act 1988.

All Rights Reserved

No reproduction, copy or transmission of this publication
may be made without written permission.
No paragraph of this publication may be reproduced,
copied or transmitted save with the written permission of the publisher, or in
accordance with the provisions
of the Copyright Act 1956 (as amended).

Any person who commits any unauthorised act in relation to
this publication may be liable to criminal
prosecution and civil claims for damage.

A CIP catalogue record for this title is
available from the British Library.

ISBN: 978-1-78830-291-3

First Published in 2019

Olympia Publishers
60 Cannon Street
London
EC4N 6NP

Printed in Great Britain

Acknowledgements

I would like to thank Mrs. Rita Morgan and year 2 (2015 – 2016) of Fawley Infant School for reading these poems and giving such encouraging feedback.

My sincere thanks go to Jon McNaught who has illustrated this book with such delightful illustrations, bringing the words truly to life.

Jon McNaught is a published author of *Dockwood* (winner of an Angouleme award in 2013), *Pebble Island* and *Birchfield Close*, all published by Nobrow Press.

Jon is a personal friend and I am very grateful to him for illustrating my poems and designing the cover.

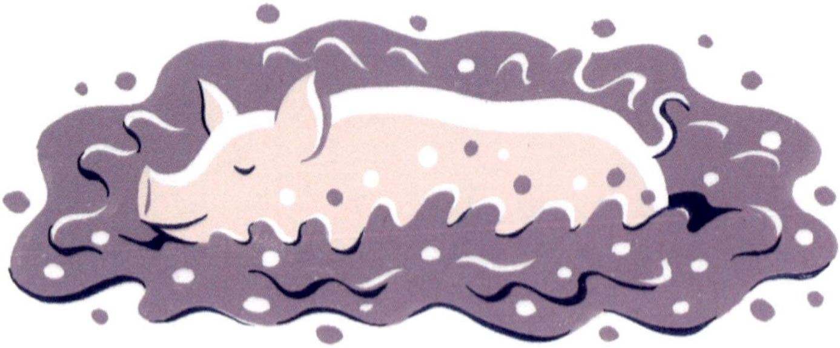

Mud, Lovely Mud!

Now Nellie was a big fat pig
She used her nose the mud to dig
She liked it best when it was wet
Her piglets she would just forget!

She'd flick her tail and flop her ears
Not listening to her piglet's jeers
And if a puddle she could find
She'd wallow with her fat behind!

The sticky mud brought her such ease
Covering her trotters and her knees.
Her piglets could not understand
Why Nellie thought it, oh, so grand!

Oh! said the farmer, here comes Nellie
Covered in mud up to her belly!
Out comes the hose, giving a good spray
Nellie grunts, he has ruined her day!

The piglets tho' thought this great fun
As the farmer hosed their big fat mum
Clean water washed away her pride!
But tomorrow in the mud she'd slide!

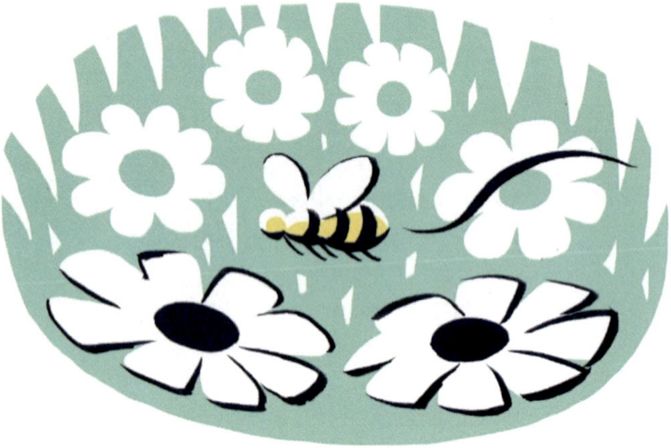

Tea Time

Now did you invite the Bee to tea?
Yes, but she says she's a busy Bee!
I'll put some flowers on the table
Then she'll come by if she is able.

As the sun wakes, she flies from the hive
Into each flower she takes a dive
Collecting pollen to take away
Back and forth throughout the day.

In the hive are many Bees
Making honey with perfect ease
Soft and gooey, so easy to spread
So, we can have honey on our bread!

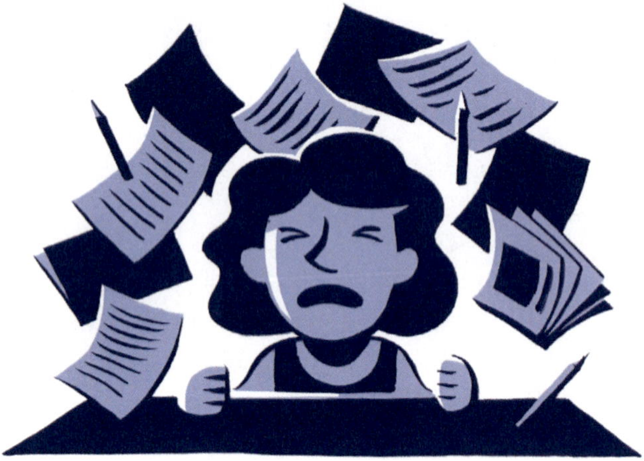

Temper! Temper!

She stamped her foot, her lips did pout
She took a deep breath, then did shout
Each time she was told what to do
Off the handle she quickly flew!

In school one day the teacher said,
Put Maths away, we'll read instead.
But being told what to do, fled
Straight back home and into bed!

Oh dear! Said Mother, this can't go on
Such temper tantrums are so wrong.
The doctor said, She should be sold
But now she is as good as gold!

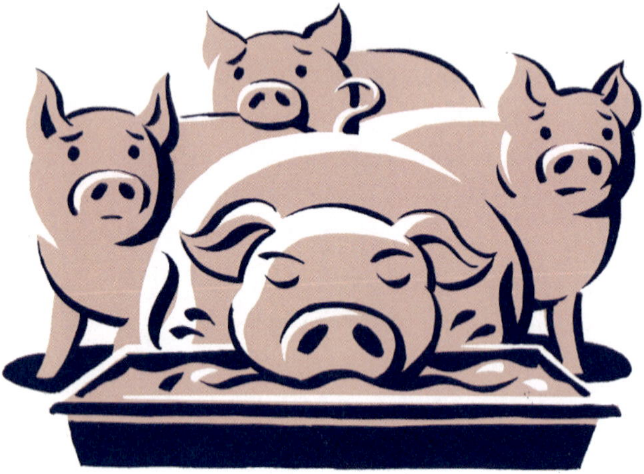

The Bully

Four little piglets living on the farm
Safe with their mother, keeping them from harm.
One of the piglets, always very bold
Often pushed the others out in the cold.
When it was lunchtime, in would go his snout
Grunting, pushing, keeping the others out.
Stop, said Mother, that isn't very kind
Do it again and I'll nip your behind!

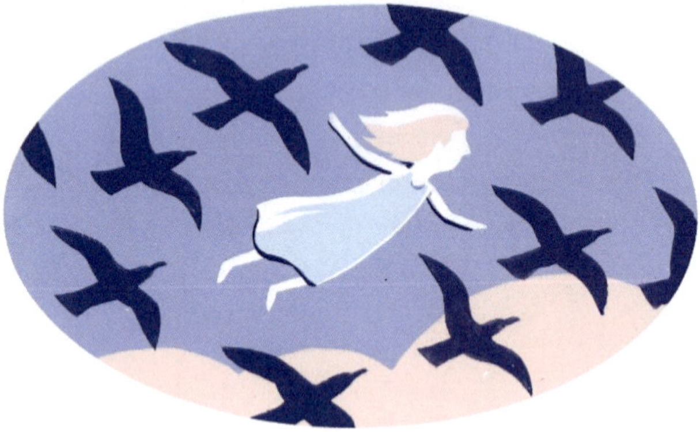

Belinda

Belinda wasn't very tall
In fact, she was extremely small
So, when she couldn't reach to see
She'd climb upon her father's knee.

One day she climbed the garden gate
To look around. But 'twas too late
A gust of wind came rushing by
Lifting Belinda way up high!

Her calls for help just went unheard
So flapped her arms just like a bird.
Realising that she could fly
She flew way up into the sky.

Such fun, and, oh, no longer small
Nothing hidden, she could see it all!
Through the clouds Belinda sped
Then with a bump, woke up in bed!

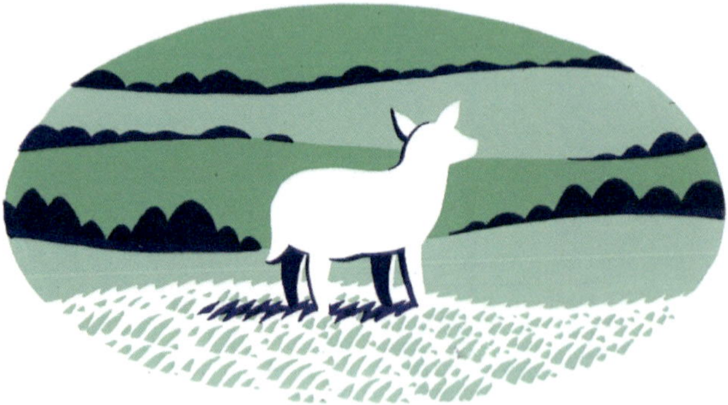

Lost Lamb

Oh, little lamb, where have you gone?
You are so small, not very strong.
Your mother's bleating all day long
Can't you hear her sad, sad song?

Little lamb, you've wandered away
Whatever made you want to stray?
You have no friends with whom to play
So please come back to us today!

Mother sheep has a broken heart
She did not want you both to part
She thought that every day would start
With her wee lamb all clean and smart!

So, all you little lambs beware
There're dangers lurking everywhere.
Stay safe and close to Mother's care.
Until you're older, stay right there!

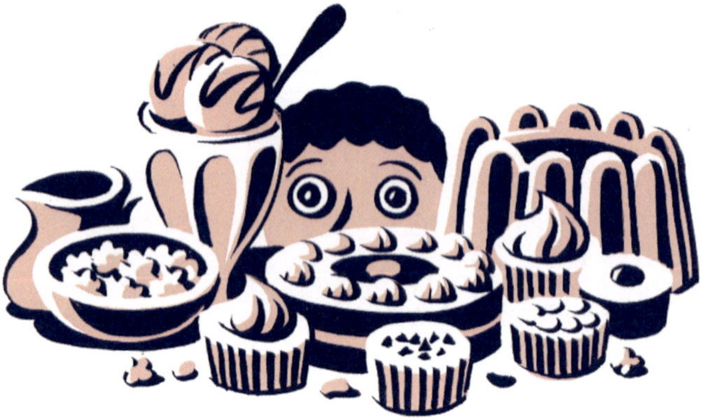

Oh Dear William

Now William really liked to eat
He slipped from his bed, onto his feet
In search of something very sweet
He liked to give himself a treat!

Chocolate cake with cream on the top
He sat and ate the blooming lot!
Then spied the jelly, he couldn't stop
As he fed his belly, plop by plop.

A packet of biscuits on the side
One by one down his throat did slide.
He ate so much he grew quite wide
Not a crumb of food got past his eye!

He didn't heed the warning to stop
Just chomped and chewed, not caring a jot!
Then suddenly. As if he'd been shot
Exploded with a very loud POP!

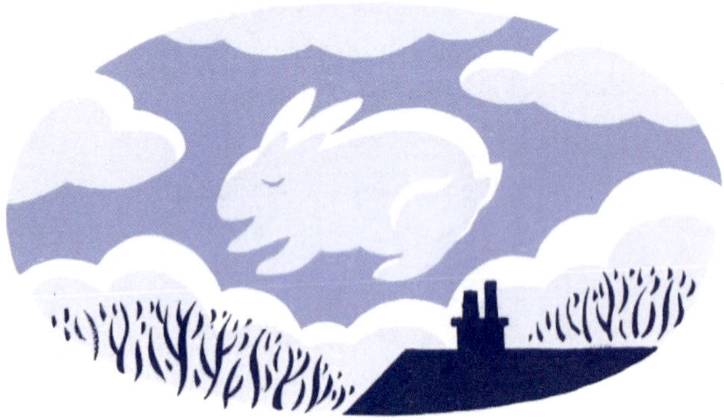

Gone but not Forgotten!

He's small and white with pink eyes and a pink nose
He is called Samson, that's the name I chose
Two big ears and whiskers stretching wide
A little mouth with big white teeth inside.

He has a smart hutch that's cosy and warm
And hops around on the green grassy lawn
For special treats he likes carrots to crunch
And often has lettuce served for his lunch.

He's warm and soft when I give him a hug
He loves to nestle in my arms, all snug
I tell him about the day spent in school
He never speaks, but listens to it all!

Then one morning when I went to his hutch
He didn't seem to want very much.
He stayed in the corner, hiding away
I made him comfortable with extra hay.

Big splashy tears falling as I cried
So sad that my friend Samson had died
No more will we play or share together
But I won't forget him, never, never!

In the garden I will find a nice spot
Among the roses where it's not too hot.
A cross marks the place where Samson is laid
So I can remember the times when we played.

I Can't Fly!

Mother Blackbird laid her eggs, one, two, three
Her nest hidden deep within the yew tree.
She turned her eggs daily and kept them warm
Popped out at times to dig worms from the lawn.

Early one day a gentle tapping was heard
Shells cracked open, 'tis the birth of a bird.
Now both parents must search for their food
Three little chicks are in hungry mood!

They grew big and strong on worms, flies and bugs
For a special treat some big juicy slugs!
Their feathers have grown, time to leave the nest
And put their new wings to a flying test.

But one of the chicks said, I can't fly
Come said Mother you really must try.
It isn't safe to stay on the ground
You really must learn to fly around.

I'm frightened; everything's so big and high
I'm really not up to learning to fly!
Come said the mother, we'll do it together
Open your wings and trust each new feather.

He flapped and bounced, then upward flew
Gaining more height as his confidence grew.
Well done, said his mum, the family cheer
We are so proud you've mastered your fear!

Thread Bear!

There was once a young bear, whose name was Fred
He was covered in fur, except for his head
His friends, they teased him for his lack of hair
How can you call yourself a proper bear?

They always teased him when the sun shone bright
They said his head looked like a shining light!
They even teased him when the rain poured down
As it made him close his eyes and frown.

I'm unhappy and lonely, said the bear!
Friends just laugh at me; they really don't care.
I will go and hide where nobody sees
Where nobody's around to laugh and tease.

Into the unknown, he drifted away
Past rocks and streams, seeking somewhere to stay.
He was hungry and cold; his paws were sore
He sat by a tree and did gently snore.

Out popped a mouse. Oh! I beg your pardon
I didn't expect a bear in my garden
I'm pleased to meet you; will you stay long?
I'd like a friend who is handsome and strong.

Do you mean me? said the bear with surprise
Oh yes! said the mouse with delighted cries.
You're a very fine bear, please stay with me
I would so enjoy your good company.